ISBN 978-0-483-73165-3
PIBN 10080270

For support please visit www.forgottenbooks.com

A

REVIEW

OF

THE EFFORTS AND PROGRESS

OF

NATIONS,

DURING THE LAST TWENTY-FIVE YEARS.

BY J. C. L. DE SISMONDI.

TRANSLATED FROM THE FRENCH,

BY PETER S. DUPONCEAU.

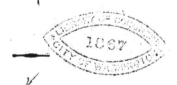

PHILADELPHIA:

HARRISON HALL, 64, SOUTH FOURTH-STREET.

R. Wright, Printer.

. . . . .

1825.

Note by the Editor of the Port Folio.

The following Translation was prepared for the Port Folio. For the accommodation of readers who are not subscribers to that journal, a few copies have been printed in the form of a pamphlet. In this form the original came from Paris to the hands of Mr. Duponceau, who kindly obliged us with this translation.

THE TRANSLATOR'S PREFACE.

THE name of the author of the following essay, is alone sufficient to recommend it to the American public. Were it anonymously published, it would still sufficiently recommend itself; for it is impossible after perusing it, not to perceive that it is the production of a man of no ordinary genius, who is thoroughly master of his subject. The mind and the pen of SISMONDI discover themselves in every line of this vivid picture of the recent progress and advancement of mankind. It is a moral *panorama* of the whole world, reduced to the compass of a few pages. It is a panorama of *time* as well as of *space*; it spreads out before the reader the first quarter of a new century which announced itself as pregnant with the most important events, and which has fulfilled its promise. Well may we say with the great man who ushered it into the world, " that the nineteenth century is not like any of those that preceded it."

The French revolution had held up to mankind the delusive hope of universal and unbounded freedom, which, like Mahomet's religion, was to be established and spread abroad by scenes of devastation, and by means destructive of its object. At the beginning of this century, while that experiment was in its full career, an extraordinary man appeared, who undertook to stop the revolutionary chariot in its wayward course; he took his seat undaunted upon the furious whirlwind; but instead of firmly and gently guiding it into the plain and obvious path of knowledge, liberty, and virtue, he gave it another headlong direction, in which he kept it for sometime with astonishing success; but in the end was precipitated by the united force of Europe, combined to restore what they called legitimate order and tranquillity to the world. The consequences of these convulsions have been gradually displaying themselves within the last ten years, and a magnificent spectacle has been opening within this period to the view of the present generation, and the wonder of posterity.

Whatever immediate causes speculative men may be pleased to assign to the various revolutions that we have witnessed, there is one which has been at work for more than two centuries, and to which all other secondary causes have been subservient. The floods of light which, since the discovery of the art of printing, have been diffused over the earth, have raised a new and universal monarch, who, seated on an imperishable throne, is henceforth to govern mankind. This monarch is *Public Opinion*. It is in vain to deny his power; the proofs of it are too evident to be doubted. It is he who effected the religious reformation; who gave to Great Britain her free constitution; who spread its most valuable principles over this vast continent; separated by means of them these states from the mother country; threw back from hence upon Europe the light which the new world had received from it, and which after once more agitating the old hemisphere, recoiled with double vigour upon the new, and filled the land of Columbus with independent republican states.

Yet in Europe, the old sovereigns, untaught by the experience of ages, are still waging a feeble war against this immense Colossus, to whom they are doomed at last to submit. This essay contains a lively picture of the various successes of this warfare within the last twenty-five years.—The author shows how public opinion has hitherto resisted all the efforts that have been made to destroy it; how it has advanced, is advancing, and is likely to conquer in the end. In England, it has been found unassailable; in France, while encroachments were making in various quarters upon constitutional liberty, the freedom of the press has suddenly blazed forth and illumined the whole atmosphere. He shows that although in Germany, Spain, and Italy, the efforts of the retrograde party appear to have been more successful, yet that the lights of those great nations have been only smothered, not extinguished; he points to Greece, to glorious Greece, as a proof of the vanity of the attempts that are making to put out a flame, which, while it appears to be subdued in one quarter, is still bursting out with greater splendour in another; and at last he cheers the hopes of the friends of liberty and of mankind, with the noble spectacle which this favoured continent for the first time exhibits since the creation of the world, that of A WHOLE REPUBLICAN HEMISPHERE.

In the back ground he shadows out another continent, situated between Asia and America, whose destinies can only be viewed at a long distance, but which promises to be another great asylum of knowledge, virtue, and liberty.

Such is the cheering and interesting picture which Mr. SISMONDI offers to the view of his European readers. I have thought that it would not be less so to Americans; particularly as the United States occupy in it a distinguished place, and are delineated there by no unfriendly hand.

This essay is extracted from the *Revue Encyclopedique* for last January:—a literary journal, published monthly at Paris, which is well known in the United States, but not as much, perhaps, as it deserves to be. It is undoubtedly the best of the kind published on the continent of Europe, and perhaps elsewhere. It is not on the same plan with the English Reviews, and therefore it cannot be well compared with them; at the same time, I cannot help observing, that it is entirely free from that flippant style, and sometimes vulgar obloquy, which too often disgraces some of the British journals. Justice also compels me to say, that its reviews of scientific and literary works are always what they profess to be, and that the reader who expects a critical and impartial analysis of a book, is not disappointed by finding in lieu of it a dissertation by the nominal reviewer, sometimes compiled from Encyclopedias and elementary works on the subject treated of by the author pretended to be reviewed, and sometimes even on topics but distantly connected with it.

The *Revue Encyclopedique* proceeds on a quite different system. It contains but few reviews, properly so called, that is to say, disquisitions in which the book reviewed is analysed and criticised fully and at large; this honor is reserved for the most distinguished works, and it cannot be supposed that many will appear of that description in the course of a single month. Of the mass of other writings notices are given, the length of which is proportioned to the merit of the work.* Sometimes, indeed, these come very near to a full review, but as they are printed in a different part of the journal, and in a different type, they are only entitled to be considered as notices. The result of this mode of proceeding is, that the reader finds in this compilation an account of every thing that appears in the literary world upon every subject, and at the end of every month can take a complete view of the progress of the human mind. The last part of the journal consists of literary and scientific news from every part of the globe, among which are recorded all the recent inventions and discoveries, and every thing else that can tend to the benefit of mankind.

Such is the plan on which the *Revue Encyclopedique* is and has been conducted for several years, under the

---

* This plan has been adopted by our own excellent North American Review; at the end of each number there is a department of *critical notices,* in which works of lesser importance are analysed more or less at length, or simply noticed according to their merits.—*Translator.*

direction of M. JULLIEN, a gentleman of distinguished talents, assisted by a number of the most eminent men in every branch of literature and science. Among those are to be found the well known names of Brogniart, the two Champollions, Chaptal, Coquebert Montbret, Dupin, de Gerando, Lanjuinais, Magendie, Orfila, Say, Segur, Sismondi, and many others, all more or less distinguished in the literary and scientific world. Its political principles are those of constitutional freedom, or what are called in Europe, *liberal principles.* Although living under a monarchy, the editors of this journal treat republics and and the republican system with proper respect.

Indeed, as Americans, we owe a debt of gratitude to the conductors of the *Revue,* which I feel happy to have it in my power thus publicly to acknowledge. They seldom miss an opportunity of noticing the gradual improvement of this country, and their reviews of American works (which are very frequent) are written in a spirit of candour, and I might even say of partiality, highly flattering to us. No sarcastic reflections are thrown out against us, no discouraging observations, no invidious comparisons between the state of literature in this country and in Europe; on the contrary, the reviewers seem anxious to exhibit American productions to the best advantage, and to place us on a footing with the other members of the republic of letters. No latent merit escapes their observation, and praise is sure to be bestowed, where in any degree it appears to be deserved. And as if they could not sufficiently show the respect which they entertain for our nation, they invariably place it at the head of all others in their notices of foreign works. Not that they mean by this to intimate that the United States are entitled to any scientific or literary pre-eminence; but they have fallen on this delicate method to encourage us to persevere in our endeavours to reach the summit of literature and science, by keeping the goal constantly in our view.

I have long wished for an opportunity to express the feeling which I know to be entertained wherever the facts are known, for the liberal treatment which our country and literature have received from the literati of the continent of Europe; particularly of France and Germany. If this little effusion should have the good fortune to reach any of them, they will know that their kindness has not been lavished upon an ungrateful people, and that their friendly conduct towards us is justly appreciated.

We were once colonies, under subjection to an European power. Our literary emancipation did not follow close upon our political independence. We have long worn shackles which we are gradually throwing off, and are beginning to set up in the literary world for ourselves! Our first efforts required friendly encouragement; we have received it from quarters whence we had the least right to expect it, and we feel grateful towards those who have not disdained to regard our infant productions with a favourable eye. The best and the only way in which we can properly requite these favours, is by exerting ourselves to deserve them more. The gradual but visible progress which American literature has made within the last ten years, is a pledge of future exertions, which I hope will be aided by frequent translations of such excellent models, as that which I now lay before the public.

A

REVIEW

OF THE

EFFORTS AND PROGRESS OF NATIONS.

It has pleased the Roman Catholic Church to distinguish the year that we are just now entering upon, by the celebration of a jubilee: abandoning the secular festivals which the greatest number of the faithful did not live to see, it has considered the fourth part of a century as a sufficiently important portion of the life of man, to require all men to pause at this period, to reflect on and review the past. It is a fit moment to acknowledge the errors that have been committed, to examine the progress that has been made, and to seek, in the remembrance of past efforts, fresh hopes for the future. Those who wish for the perfection, or at least the melioration of the human species, who ardently desire its further progress in knowledge, virtue, and liberty; those who are anxious to see man always improving the faculties which raise him above the brutes; his conscience, his intelligence, his will;—such persons will do well to celebrate this jubilee with

B

the Church of Rome. They, also, will find it beneficial to take a retrospective view of the past, to examine the course which they have run, to repent of their errors, to confirm their faith in the truths already known, and lastly, to derive fresh hopes from the lessons of experience.

The first twenty-five years of the nineteenth century have passed away; they had a character peculiar to themselves; a single interest exclusively occupied them: that of the struggle between two opinions which divide the world, and dispose of the power of nations. The one tends to make the human species march forward, the other to keep it stationary, or make it trace back its steps. In various countries, each of those opinions has in turns been victorious; violent revolutions, overthrowings of empires, have, within this quarter of a century, signalized the alternate triumphs of the two parties. They are still in array before each other; the issue of their contest is yet uncertain; and although we are far from pretending to remain neutral between them, we think that we may, without bitterness, without partiality, and without any hostility in our language, take a fair view of their respective positions.

And first, in the midst of various fatal events, and of several discouraging experiments, it is a ground of hope for the friends of humanity, that the cause of this struggle is at last clearly defined, the character of both parties, their aims, and their hopes, are fully developed, and no longer susceptible of any ambiguity. It has not always been thus during the twenty-five years that we have travelled over. Each party has played the tyrant in its turn; each, in the intoxication of power, has braved the light of reason, the dictates of morality, and the proud feeling of liberty; virtuous men have been seen arrayed from conscientious motives, under opposite banners; both were animated by the same desire of saving all that ennobles man, of checking revolutionary or despotic fanaticism, of preserving civilization, virtue, liberty, which it appeared to them that their adversaries were treading under foot. Men have not different opinions on the value of these treasures; they differ only as to the means of obtaining them, the character by which they may be distinguished, and the alloy with which they are sometimes debased; but no one has ever thought of repelling from himself knowledge, virtue, or freedom. "We are fighting for liberty," said a republican soldier to the imperialists. "And we," answered an Austrian officer, "do you think we are fighting in order to be slaves?"

It was for a long time a source of error, to make a distinction between the progressive faculties of man, as if the whole interest of the present generation depended on liberty, or knowledge, or virtue; whereas, on the contrary, they are closely united and almost undivisible. Man must be enlightened, in order to distinguish good from evil: he must be virtuous, in order to adhere to the former; and free, that he may effect his choice; but the same knowledge which must direct his moral election, will point out to him all the other good things that he may desire, and all the means of obtaining them; and each progressive step of his intelligence will produce a corresponding advancement of virtue and liberty. A great cause of ambiguity and confusion has been done away since the friends of humanity have made known the intimate connexion which exists between these three developments of the human faculties. Then the retrograde party was compelled to take its stand, and must have said: "We believe knowledge, virtue and liberty to be good things; we believe that from them results an increase of riches, population and power, which also are good things; but we want those good things for ourselves alone:" while the progressive party have answered: "Because we believe all those things to be good, we want them for all mankind; for, what we are seeking is the greatest good of the greatest number."

Language has been so much perverted by the tools of power, and the words of which it is composed have been so much employed in sophistical reasonings, that however clearly the question which divides the world may be now defined, it will not be impossible for an artful orator to involve it in doubt, and to confound simple minds by words skilfully put together; but facts are now before the world which may explain the two principles, and serve as a standard to the two opinions.

The United States of America represent the progressive tendency which the promoters of one of these opinions are striving to give to mankind. Since their emancipation, and particularly during the last quarter of a century, their government has shown no hesitation in its firm resolution to march forward, to favour with all its might the progress of knowlege, virtue and liberty; and the rapid increase of the prosperity of the United States has surpassed all that has ever been known on the face of the earth. In order to judge of this, we must not lose sight of the point from which they started. The founders of the colonies were fugitives of all political and religious sects, each of which had been persecuted in its turn; they carried with them the germs of every animosity, they were filled with deep resentment, fraught with fanaticism of every description, and disposed to every kind of exaggeration. For a long time they were reunited by the scum of the English population, by individuals transported for their crimes; at a later period, their country became the refuge of fortune-seekers, of intriguers and adventurers of all nations; the colonies received from the governments of Europe the most fatal of all institutions— slavery; a part* of their population is dispersed in forests, or in immense prairies, beyond the reach of courts of justice, or of social protection. With such elements, the Ame-

---

* The original says, "the greatest part," which is evidently a mistake. The portion of our population so situated, is, on the contrary, very small, compared to the whole. *Translator.*

ricans would have been, under our European governments, the most vicious of all people; they are entitled, on the contrary, to rank amongst the most virtuous. There are few nations among whom the sent\ 't of what is right, just and honourable, is more univer\ _ead; where crimes are more rare; where domestic virtues are more in honour; where religion, which, however, has no other sanction than every man's conscience, exercises a more general influence. No doubt there are yet to be found traces of the stain which their founders fixed upon them; but they are every day rapidly disappearing. In the same manner, in the career of intelligence, it must not be forgotten that the Americans are but just beginning; they must have been colonists, agriculturers, mechanics, traders, before they had leisure to devote to the pursuits of philosophy, or literature. We cannot yet expect from them those masterly productions which at once charm and enlighten mankind; but they have had the sagacity to appropriate to themselves all the arts and sciences of Europe; they have spread, over the whole of their population, more reason, more positive knowledge, more aptness to imbibe correct ideas, than is found in the mass of the people of any of the old nations of Europe. The liberty of America has developed and strengthened itself with its knowledge and virtue. No citizen of any other country has so many rights and so many securities; and those rights have never produced the abuses with which we are constantly threatened; no popular commotions, no insurrections, no civil wars; they have enjoyed perfect security in the midst of perfect liberty. What is now the result of this treble progression? At the beginning of the present century, the American population amounted to four or five millions; they are now eleven millions.* At the

---

* The president of the United States, in his late inaugural speech, estimates our present population at twelve millions. *Translator.*

beginning of this century, their towns were yet small and poor; they now vie in extent, in population, and in beauty, with the capitals of Europe. At the beginning of this century, the United States bore with difficulty the weight of their national debt; now their funds are no longer quoted at the London Exchange; their debt is reduced to almost nothing, and they are indebted only to themselves. At the beginning of this century, their commerce, their industry, and even their agriculture, were fed by British capitals: at present, notwithstanding the immensity of their undertakings, their own capitals are sufficient to support them; they overflow in the trade of Europe and India, they throng in the states of America that were lately Spanish, and impart to them all the arts of civilization. This is what the Americans have done during the last twenty-five years; they have advanced and are advancing: is it then to be wondered at that we should wish to advance likewise?

Unfortunately, it is not difficult to find, also, examples of the retrograde tendency. In order to offend as little as possible those who do not like to hear home truths, we shall chuse one of those examples at a distance from ourselves, in a country, the government of which does not disguise its intentions by hypocritical language. That country, situated between the three monarchies of Europe, that are styled empires, belongs properly to neither; but all three, by their protection, keep it in the situation in which it now is, and are determined that it shall so continue. It includes *Moldavia*, *Wallachia*, *Bulgaria* and *Servia*, four principalities on which nature has bestowed the richest soil in Europe, the most temperate climate, the noblest river, and the most ancient commercial road, that fomerly connected the East and the West, and the civilization of Constantinople with that of Germany and France. But that country, where Providence had implanted the germ of every kind of prosperity calculated to produce

happiness and glory, has constantly been under the retrograde system; and since Trajan, who made it flourish, since
Charlemagne, who restored the communication between the
two empires, it has never ceased to pursue a retrograde course.
In those unfortunate provinces, there is no safety for persons,
nor for property; there is neither commerce, nor industry,
nor agriculture; the population is reduced below one twentieth of what the soil could maintain; it is more savage and more
unhappy than the wild beasts that share with it the products
of the *valley of the Danube*. There is no country, (particularly Bulgaria and Servia), whence liberty, knowledge, and virtue, have been more carefully excluded; the peasantry are *serfs*,
and their masters do not even protect them as their property; instruction there is impossible, for their language is not
written; virtue is entirely unknown: it is not to be sought for
in the peasantry;—men who have no rights to enjoy, have no
duties to perform; and as to the noblemen, or *Boyards*, as
they are called, the low debauchery of the men, and the
shameless profligacy of the women, form a shocking contrast
to the luxury with which they endeavour to surround themselves. The state of war, which for ages has continued without interruption in those principalities, occasions to their
neighbours frequent losses, and requires from them constant
watchfulness. Those neighbours are the most powerful mo-
narchs of Europe: yet they have never called a congress;
they never have even availed themselves of the influence
secured to them by treaties, in order to stop the effusion of
human blood, and put an end to the lawless state of society
which exists in those countries. What is now the result
which they have obtained from such a state of things? It is
this:—To whatever degree of oppression the Wallachian or
Moldavian peasant may be subjected, there is no apprehen-
sion that he will rise in rebellion: you may *impale* him, but

you cannot compel him to defend himself. As to us, who have not the same interest, it is well now and then to cast our eyes on the Wallachian and Moldavian peasantry; if such is the end of the retrograde movement, surely we ought not to be disposed to retrace our steps.

Let us not suffer ourselves to be misled by those who employ other words to express the two opposite tendencies: those words have exercised a lamentable influence on the quarter of a century which we have just passed through, and have produced a great number of errors. The two parties have deceived themselves by assuming principles which did not well express their real sentiments; some have laid down, as an axiom, the principle of the *sovereignty of the people,* but this *dogma* (for such it is in fact) constantly led them into error.* If they were obliged to give the name of *people* to the aggregation of all men, if they acknowledged in all an equal right to govern, they themselves opposed the greatest obstacle to the progress of society, for the ignorant mass is far more numerous than the enlightened part of the community, it does not know what is good, and frequently rejects it; and the sovereign multitude has not shown itself less disposed to *retrograde* than despots. The adversaries of this party have opposed to this dogma that of *legitimacy,* which they attempted to make the foundation of the sovereign power. The inventor of this doctrine did not mean to make it the standard of the retrograde system throughout Europe; he only thought of France; and considering as tainted every power derived from revolutionary violence, he sought the right where it was before force was exercised; he recognized it in the sovereign as well as in the subject, by its most permanent sign, its regular and quiet transmission

---

* It must not be forgotten that this is written under a monarchical government. *Translator.*

through several successive generations; in short, what jurists call *prescription*. But when the retrograde party laid hold of this term, they applied it in the most absurd manner to other countries and to other governments; even to those in which the principle of legitimacy had been most flagrantly violated. For, have they forgotten, who insist on legitimacy for Germany and Italy, that the legitimate constitution of the Holy Roman Empire, that which existed there prior to the revolution, founded on treaties, on a regular and quiet transmission of rights, in short, on prescription, gave to those two countries an elective sovereign, and a body of electors, three of whom were elective in their turn? That constitution has been entirely subverted; while all the rights, all the claims which this party contends for, are founded on the Revolution. The rest of Europe would not be less embarrassed to show in the powers to which they are now subjected, the character of legitimacy: almost every where the ancient laws, on which power was formerly founded, have been abolished.*

After all, the partisans of the *retrograde system* need only a *watchword*, with or without meaning, to recognize each other by, while the friends of the *progressive system* are bound to use more precision. The dogma of the sovereignty of the people can serve but to perplex and confound them.† It is useless to go back to the origin of power, it must be considered as a *fact;* it exists; it has been instituted, therefore it has duties to perform: those duties are the advancement of the ends of human society, the happiness of the governed, their progress in virtue, in knowledge, in liberty; the fulfilment of these duties gives to governments the character of legitimacy, and is the noblest evidence of their title. Those

---

* Witness Genoa, Venice, the Ionian Islands, Malta, part of Saxony, Poland, Sweden, Holland, Belgium, &c.—*Sismondi*.

† We find no such perplexity or confusion in this country.—*Translator*.

C

duties are common to all, they may be fulfilled by all, whatever may be the form of the government. All forms, it is true, are not equally calculated to guaranty their fulfilment; but we must be contented with imperfect securities; those have not yet been found which could be adapted to all countries, and protect the just and reasonable rights of men united in society.

Having thus endeavoured to show, what is the object of the struggle in which mankind has been engaged during this quarter of a century, we shall now proceed to estimate its results. No doubt, during that period, the human race has experienced great misfortunes and cruel catastrophes; yet it may still applaud itself for the progress it has made.

FRANCE, of course, is uppermost in our thoughts; France gave the impulse to all the other nations; France has dearly paid for her experience; conquering or conquered, she has seen professed, in her name, the most opposite doctrines; and she was forced to submit to the governments which were given to her by all the extreme parties. No doubt she may express her regret; no doubt she may still entertain fears; no doubt she may complain that recent periods have been strongly marked with a retrograde character; but if she places herself at the distance of twenty-five years back, and from that point of view considers what has taken place within this quarter of a century, she will perceive that she has gained more than she has lost. Ideas of justice and public order have been developed and strengthened; political knowledge has been universally spread; the two parties have in a great measure abandoned their prejudices; the classes which repelled constitutional forms have become attached to the power which they have acquired under them, even while they abused it. Morality, it is true, has suffered by the progress of hypocrisy and venality; knowlege, by the opposi-

tion which has been made to, the best mode of public instruction,* and liberty, by encroachments which it is unnecessary
to recapitulate here. The efforts of corruption have been directed at the same time, as they always are, against the heart,
against the mind, against the free exercise of the will; but
the progress of prosperity has restored more to the French,
than the abuse of power has taken from them. The advancement of every kind of industry, the general welfare, and the
national wealth, have raised again the national character; for
citizens can only feel their independence, and their moral
dignity, when they are above want: the late improvement
of the people's circumstances has given to all classes a greater desire of information, and more leisure to acquire it. And,
lastly, by way of compensation for the part of her rights that
she has lost, France is in possession of the LIBERTY OF THE
PRESS; this valuable privilege secures the empire of thought,
and of elevated sentiments, and is, consequently, the most
powerful engine towards the improvement of the human race.
Thus, notwithstanding her many reverses, France is in a progressive state of melioration. She has marched gloriously
forward.

GERMANY has experienced a shock not less severe than
that which visited France. During the greater part of this
quarter of a century, her fields were the theatre of the war;
she has seen all her institutions overthrown, all her states have
received new denominations, new laws, or new boundaries;
and if the epithet *legitimate* is applicable only to the order
of things which preceded the convulsions of this quarter of
a century, there remains nothing in that country entitled to
it. But France made her own revolutions, while Germany only yielded to foreign impulses; therefore, instead of

---

* The Lancasterian System.—*Translator.*

advancing, she has retrograded. At the beginning of this century, each state was endeavouring to amend its own institutions, to introduce into them somewhat more of liberty, a few
more securities; each government wished to acquire the love
of its subjects, which, in the common danger, was its only
source of strength. The people, confiding in their princes,
and in return obtaining their confidence, was proceeding 'forward in concert with them, with slow but sure steps. The
universities were full of life and spirit; it was on the progress
of science, on the development of the intellectual powers, that
Germany wished to settle the foundation of her dignity; the
greatest freedom existed in the department of public instruction. Nay, more, the universities were a political power; it
was they, who after having enlightened and directed public
opinion, undertook to disseminate and make it known; the
press, saving direct questions of state policy, was almost entirely free; and the spirit of association which had taken its
birth in Germany, and which the sovereigns had strongly
encouraged, gave to the speculations of philosophers an immediate action on the mass of the people. All this has been
changed: fear, as a principle of obedience, has been substitut-
ed for affection; morality has been impaired by the encouragement given to informers and spies, and still more by great and
striking breaches of public faith, which have enriched those
who thus violated their promises; literature and science have
been checked in their noble progress; the universities have
been fettered, the press is enslaved, and associations are
punished as state offences; the ancient constitution, anomalous,
indeed, and often barbarous, but which required only amend-
ments, has been suppressed, without being replaced by any
other; yet, faulty as it was, it restrained absolute power in a
great degree; it accustomed sovereigns to speak of liberty;
it secured the rights of electors, princes and prelates, of
the immediate nobility, and of the free cities. Henceforth,

there are no rights in any manner established, and Germany has ceased to be a nation. Nothing is now to be found there but princes more or less weak or powerful, and more or less trembling on their thrones before their subjects or their neighbours. The ancient country of war and politics has no longer any weight in the balance of Europe.

ITALY has been more unfortunate than Germany. In the course of these five-and-twenty years, Italy might well have entertained the fairest hopes. Awakened at last from the torpor and effeminate corruption in which she had forgotten her enslaved situation, she had risen through military virtue and patriotism to other virtues, and by applying herself to the science of government, she had felt anew the importance of study, and had restored the former elasticity to that intelligence with which her people is so eminently endowed. In the midst of this period, her government was changed, but the country did not abandon its hopes; for, in order to obtain the co-operation of the people, the most solemn promises had been lavished, that they should participate in the progress of the age. Those promises having been forgotten, two revolutions broke out at the two extremities of Italy, and in the midst o. those national fevers, always terrible, the improvement of the Italian nation might be perceived. Their revolutions were accomplished without effusion of blood, without pillage, without insult, without violence: in both of them, the presumptive heir to the throne put himself at the head of the reformers, and if this double experience is for ever to dissuade nations from *royal revolutions,* it also proves that the Italians knew how to unite gratitude for the past, with hope for the future. In the struggle with foreigners which followed, the retrograde system prevailed: Italy was punished for her wishes and her efforts by public executions: her proscribed citizens sought an asylum in all the cities of Europe; they were men distinguished by their knowledge, their virtues, and the sacrifices they had made for the happiness of their country: they were noblemen of high rank, who had devoted their fortunes and their talents to the introduction of new branches of useful industry, which they brought from other countries, to the founding of public schools, institutions for the deaf and dumb, and the publication of scientific journals. Military tribunals, police commissioners, still more terrible, annihilated all legal guarantees, made terror sit heavy on all classes of society: morality was attacked by the examples given of the contempt of oaths, by the encouragement offered to informers and domestic traitors, by the state of despair into which the minds of men were thrown, which made them seek to forget the public misfortunes by indulging in luxury and vice; knowledge was attacked, by taking away the means of instruction, by the suspension or suppression of lectures in the universities, by the proscription of foreign books, and the mutilation of those which were published in the country; war was declared against intellectual pursuits as openly as against liberty: the liberal sciences and the liberal arts shared in the proscription that was denounced against liberal ideas. Nevertheless, we believe that in the midst of these frightful reverses, Italy is still in a progressive state: institutions are corrupting, but reason is expanding; the nation is advancing, in spite of the efforts of power to drive it backwards: there is in Italy, at the present moment, more misfortune and more oppression, but there is also more virtue, more knowledge and more patriotism than there was in 1800. In proportion as it is compressed, the Italian mind seems to have acquired a greater elasticity.

The state of SPAIN is still more dreadful. This proudest of all nations was intoxicated by the applause which Europe bestowed upon her resistance to Napoleon. Beyond the

Pyrenees, fanaticism had allied itself to liberty, for the defence of the country: in the rest of Europe, the partisans of the two systems, progressive and retrograde, had celebrated, in concert, successes for which the Spaniards were still more indebted to their climate and their poverty than to their bravery or their talents. All the passions were excited in the Peninsula, but they were subject to two opposite impulses. Spain could neither remain in her ancient barbarism under the yoke of every abuse and disgraced by every kind of ignominy, nor could she proceed forward, such was the disunion between the different classes of the nation. She, however, attempted a revolution; it was not soiled by any crime, neither was it signalized by any great national development of ability or talent. The only class which had made some progress, wished to advance still further; but the great mass of the population, which had been kept for ages in habits of ferocity, ignorance and abject dependence, repelled with stupid horror the advancement of morality, knowledge, and liberty. The populace never can comprehend the benefits that are intended for it until after it has been in the enjoyment of them: the revolutionists should, therefore, in the first place, have enabled it to participate in the benefits of the revolution, but they had neglected to secure the means of doing so. Confounding the equilibrium which preserves institutions with the power that establishes them, they had annihilated the government without daring to take it into their own hands: they kept the prince in subjection, but had not reserved to themselves any means to satisfy the people. As soon as they were attacked, they succumbed, because they had not a nation to back them; and that populace which they could not enlist on their side, now reigns over them. Let us not be deceived; Spain has now reached that period of the French revolution, which we cannot look upon without horror, the reign of all that is the most abject and the most ferocious in the nation; but she has come to it by the opposite road to that which the French followed; the tyranny of the lowest class is the result of a counter-revolution made by the ministers of kings, under the pretence, and no doubt with the intent, of serving the royal cause. They speak of a *furious Camarilla*,* their fury is that of cowardice. The court sycophants, conscious of their insignificance, have sought every where for an auxiliary force, but they have found no other than the blind fury of the populace: they endeavour to lean upon that wretched rabble; they flatter them; they boast of sharing their passions; but it is doing too much honor to the *Camarilla* to suppose that they have passions; they are what they have always been, intriguing and abject before the power of the moment, and that power, they well know, no longer inhabits palaces, but dwells in lanes and blind alleys.

Nevertheless, the triumph of the *retrogrades* has been so complete in Spain, that they themselves are frightened at their own success. All that was formerly respected is now trodden under foot; religion is subjected to a disgrace from which she had until now been exempt; she is called in as auxiliary to the police, and the depositaries of the secrets of *confession* are ordered to give information of the most private thoughts of their *penitents*. It is strange that the court of Rome never should have protested against this sacrilegious ordinance: never was a more fatal blow given to her power. Besides, the *terrorist* government of Spain disgraces the magistrates as well as the priests; every where the courts of justice are called upon to issue proscriptions in lieu of sentences; and authority does nothing more than echo the language of the ferocious chiefs of the factions.

---

* " A back-stairs *junta*."—A secret council of courtiers and favourites, by whom the king is governed, and whose plans are followed, in preference to those of his regular and ostensible counsellors.—*Translator.*

But, whatever grief we may feel for the condition of three il-
lustrious nations, let us not, on that account, despair of the fate
of the human race; let us not even despair of those nations
themselves; the human race is marching forward while they
are going back; it will continue to march on, it will raise
them up and carry them along in its course.

And first, ENGLAND should alone be sufficient to re-animate
our hopes; England, which has so nobly placed herself at the
head of the progressive movement of the human mind; England, which teaches us how the developments of liberty,
virtue, and knowledge, may be combined with all the ancient
institutions, and the most deeply rooted habits of subordina-
tion. Let us not hearken to those morose men, who, among
a thousand brilliant qualities, can only perceive defects; neither
let us listen to those who, mistaking their jealousy for patriotism, think that they are raising France by lowering her rival
in the public estimation. We would have profited very little
by the events that we have witnessed, if we had not learned
that nations have ceased to be rivals; that they have now but
one interest, being engaged in a common struggle against
those who would wish to make them retrograde, and that consequently the progress of their neighbours is the commence-
ment of their own success.

England, on her side, has but lately learned this lesson of
the age: her cabinet, adhering to the ancient policy, of the
fallacy of which many statesmen are yet hardly convinced,
brought her to the brink of ruin, by attending to these absurd
and immoral maxims of national rivalship. Long did it act
under the persuasion that the enemies of its enemies were its
friends: and England saw at Waterloo the reins of Europe fall
from her hand. On the eve of that battle the English were
the chiefs of the coalition; the next day, they were only its
pay-masters. Those who for twenty years had been the allies
of Great Britain, gave the British cabinet to understand that,

D

being no longer in need of her assistance, they cared no more for her advice.

It was then, while groaning under the weight of an enormous debt, contracted more for the benefit of others than her own; it was in the midst of a commercial revolution which threatened the destruction of her riches, that England displayed the resources of a nation which had never ceased to develop, at the same time, her knowledge, her liberty, and her virtue. The sceptre of Europe, which she thought she had fast hold of, was broken in her hands; she grasped, in lieu of it, the torch with which she enlightens the whole of the universe. Asia, Africa, America, press forward to the scene of civilization, and for this they are indebted to the British nation.

We may, it is true, point out as defects in England, the excess of the inequality of ranks and fortunes, the corruption of elections, the increasing influence of ministers, the enormous expense of legal proceedings, by means of which the poor are in a manner excluded from courts of justice; but let it not be said that England is losing her liberty. We are far from denying the existence of abuses; we are far from wishing the postponement of reforms: those which have taken place render the others still more necessary; they exhibit, in a still more shocking point of view, the contrast between the wrecks of ancient barbarism, and the institutions of an enlightened age; but such as she is, England holds the first rank among nations, by the union of liberty, knowledge, and virtue; by her long enjoyment of those prerogatives; by the progress in all three of them, that she has not ceased to make; by the empire of opinion which becomes every day more powerful in that country; by the spreading of national education, which daily calls more and still more numerous classes of people to know, and knowing, to understand, the interests of their country; to have, in respect to those interests, a will conformable to reason and virtue, and to manifest that will. Not only England is more free than she was five-and-twenty years ago, but she understands better what liberty is, she is disposed to make a better use of it, and has become enabled to acquire a greater degree of it.

The lesser states of Europe,—SWEDEN, which can only consolidate her new government by an intimate union with the people; HOLLAND, which is endeavouring to make noble and ancient recollections accord with recent experiments; SWITZERLAND, astonished at having slumbered five centuries after the generous efforts she made to free herself from tyranny,—are all likewise animated with a progressive impulse; but, perhaps, it is not expedient for weak nations to display too broadly the advantages which they have over the strong, or to show too clearly by their example the intimate union of liberty, knowledge, and virtue, and that the development of the one, necessarily produces that of the two others.

The Colossus which sits heavy on Europe, is itself in a state of progression—RUSSIA sees increasing, with a prodigious rapidity, not only the number of her inhabitants, but their riches, their knowledge, their moral feelings, and even their rights. In the state of barbarism and absolute ignorance into which that country was plunged, it was not possible to put her immediately in possession of the prerogatives of civilized nations; it would have been dangerous to confer upon them too precipitately the rights of citizenship; but that is the reproach which *all* governments deserve the least:* nevertheless, instruction is rapidly spreading in Russia, and the government favours it; the nobility, by their hopes, by their reading, and by their travels, take part in the general course of European improvement: the peasantry have been enlighten-

---

* The author might have excepted the government of the United States.
                                                        Translator.

ed in their turn, by a collision which they had little reason to expect: as soldiers, they have overrun Europe, and have beheld the advantages which the more civilized nations enjoyed; returning home, they brought with them, as prisoners, thousands of Frenchmen, Italians, and Germans, who made the name of liberty resound in their ears; on the other hand, the government, by a hazardous experiment, is forming in its military colonies, a class of men who will have rights and force to assist them: morality must follow the progress of knowledge; in this respect, no doubt, the Russians are most backward; but if a gradual enfranchisement of the people take place, the moment will be at hand when the civil, military, and judicial organization of Russia will cease to be the most venal in the universe.

Notwithstanding her internal improvement, Russia has several times employed her strength and her influence in promoting and hastening the retrograde movement among other nations. She has been misled by a false policy, and other powers more enlightened than she is, have not been free from the same errors. Civilization may yet for some time fear the armies of Russia, but the progress itself of her strength must give reasonable hopes to the friends of humanity; because she must be advancing at the same time in the path of morality and liberty. The time is not far distant when the Russians will become a truly European nation, and when the caprice of a monarch will not be sufficient to employ them in stifling all knowledge, liberty, and virtue.

And lastly, GREECE is in Europe,—that glorious Greece, which, groaning under the most degrading and cruel oppression, sought in the first place *virtue*, by the sacrifice of all her interests to the preservation of the christian religion,— *knowledge*, in an intercourse with the European nations, and who will very soon be indebted to both for her *liberty*. Greece proves to us that the days of heroism are not at an end, and that the weakest nations, by a firm resolve, may be the arbiters of their own fate. What can be the object of those whose wishes are opposed to the success of the Greeks? Do they wish to encourage apostacy? The Turks, it is true, reward the apostate by granting to him a pardon for all the crimes he has committed, by admitting him to a share of honours and power. Do they wish that the sons and daughters of Greece should continue to be at the mercy of the Turks, in order to satiate their infamous passions? Do they wish that the only distinction allowed to the Greeks should be that of the Fanariots,* power purchased by perfidy, exercised by pillage, and soon to be lost by the fatal bow-string? Do they wish that commerce, the only means of acquiring property in Greece, should continue to be polluted by the avarice and bad faith which they themselves charge the Greeks with, and to which they have been reduced by the excess of oppression? Do they wish that, every other road to heroism being closed, no means should be left for the exercise of their courage but in the character of *klephts* or robbers? Do they wish that every distinction between right and wrong should be obliterated in the hearts of the subjects, by the venality which is known to be common to all the Turkish judges? Is it the morality of Greece that they wish to preserve, or is it her knowledge? they are the most ingenious people upon earth; they are the nation to whose ancestors we are indebted for all we know, and all we are; but since they have been under the dominion of that government, which they are now struggling to overturn, they have not added a single discovery to the intellectual riches of mankind; they have not advanced one step in the most innocent sciences, in

---

* The more ancient and wealthy Greek families, who inhabit a part of Constantinople, called the *Fanar,* and from whom are selected the Hospodars of Moldavia and Wallachia.—*Translator.*

medicine, chemistry, natural history; they have no longer any literature, academies or schools, and how could they do any thing towards the general improvement of the human race? They are driven beyond the bounds of civilization, they are not permitted to approach the threshold of those sciences of which every one of us is in possession.

But, perhaps, the Turks care little for virtue and intelligence, the noblest prerogatives of our species,—and their friends would prefer for them more substantial advantages, such as peace and wealth. Is it, then, the peace of Greece that they wish to preserve; of Greece, where the scymetar of the mussulman alone governs; where a barbarous soldiery has behaved during four centuries, and still behaves as in a town taken by storm; where large cities are reduced to heaps of ruins; where, during four hundred years, nothing has been built, nothing repaired, nothing planted, nothing cultivated; where the population does not reach the twentieth part of the number of inhabitants that the soil might maintain; where there is no possible industry for the cultivator of the land, but the pasturing of sheep and goats in the wilderness? Surely we would have been afraid to calumniate the partisans of the retrograde system, if we had before-hand supposed that they took part with the Turks, and wished to assimilate to the government of Turkey those whose defence they undertook. Europe, in fact, is unanimous in her wishes for the deliverance of the Greeks, although most of those who dispose of her forces and her treasures refuse to apply them to that object. In two countries of Europe, only, that which has the least and that which enjoys the most liberty, some public journals have expressed an opinion in favour of the Turks. As to the *Austrian Observer*, his conscience is not his own, and he must not be held accountable for the opinions he expresses. In England, on the other hand, precisely in consequence of the liberty that exists there, degrading feelings and passions find suitable organs. Since there are men who will neither have virtue, liberty or knowledge, there must also be journals, such as the *New Times,* and sometimes the *Courier*, to express their sentiments. Thus, air-holes are made in mines in order to give a free passage to mephitic exhalations.

But the progress of civilization is no longer confined to Europe: the whole universe participates in it, and within this quarter of a century, its development has been prodigious. We have already shown* how seventy millions of East Indians have begun to receive from the English East India Company the benefits of European cultivation. We will not speak here of that colony of *New South Wales*, still in its cradle, still contaminated by the impure elements of which it is composed, but which, established in a temperate climate, larger than Europe, aided by the vivifying power of England, appears as if it should one day cover its whole surface, and prove that from the refuse of the hulks may arise a free, enlightened, and virtuous nation. Neither shall we speak of the colonies destined to spread civilization over the vast continent of *Africa*, and which, from the *Cape of Good Hope* and *Siera Leone*, will gradually carry knowledge and virtue into the interior, in order to make amends for the long series of European crimes, and for the fatal consequences of the negro slave trade: their destiny is yet concealed under the veil of futurity.

The career which has been run by the new *Haytian Nation* at *St. Domingo*, is still a subject of greater triumph for humanity. There the sons of Africa have proved that they are men, that they deserve to be free, and that they know how to appreciate knowledge and virtue. A frightful crime of the Europeans transported the Africans into the islands of America; a series of crimes maintained them there in

---

* Revue Encyclopédique, tom. xxiv. p. 635.

slavery, and made them ferocious; if they also committed crimes when they burst their fetters, the whole responsibility lies upon those who forged their chains. While slavery continued at St. Domingo, immorality and ignorance were in proportion to the absolute privation of liberty. In the islands where slavery still subsists, almost all the masters are openly opposed to the marriage of their slaves, to their conversion to the Christian Religion, and to the establishment of schools. Since *Hayti* has been free, and the blacks their own masters, their eagerness for instruction has even exceeded that which they had before shown for liberty. One quarter of a century has been sufficient to transform those who were considered as cattle in the human shape into a civilized people, among whom schools are opening on all sides, where thought makes a rapid progress; where every year, in spite of the climate, an evident improvement takes place in the morals of the people; where crimes are rare; where justice is administered with promptness, and impartiality; where agriculture, industry and commerce prosper; where riches accumulate with rapidity, and where the population has increased two fold, even in the midst of the terrible wars that have accomplished and followed the emancipation. This is what *negroes* have been able to do in five and twenty years; while in the Eastern part of Europe, an all powerful government, repelling the knowledge of its neighbours, and disregarding its own experience, has detained, during four centuries, one half of its provinces in slavery, poverty and barbarism, because it is hostile to all improvements, even to those from which it derives its strength and its riches in the other half of the empire.*

The most gigantic step, however, that humanity has made

---

* Could not the same observation be applied to the conduct of another government in the *West* of Europe, towards a numerous and unfortunate class of their subjects.—*Translator.*

within the last year, is the emancipation of five great American republics, *Columbia, Buenos Ayres, Chili, Peru,* and *Mexico;* each of them surpassing in extent the space which, three centuries ago, was occupied by ancient civilization. They have just burst into light, and already their power and their riches place them on an equality with the greatest states.

In those vast regions, which, by an absurd policy, their government endeavoured to retain in ignorance, poverty and barbarism, in order to secure their obedience, every European, even from a country in alliance with Spain, who landed without permission, was declared guilty of a capital crime; every vessel in distress, which, driven by adverse winds and storms, sought an asylum in their harbours, was confiscated, and her crew confined in dungeons for life. Now the ports of both Americas, on an extent of four thousand leagues of coast, are open to all nations: they are particularly frequented by the English and the *North Americans,* whose funds give animation to their industry, and who, with all the products of the arts, disseminate among them every sort of social and useful knowledge. Formerly, no American was entrusted with power, offices were sold at Madrid to the highest bidder: now, every career is opened, and employments are given to those who make the greatest efforts and prove themselves to be best entitled to the confidence of their fellow citizens. Formerly, no university, no public school, was allowed in those countries; no book was admitted without the approbation of the inquisition, and not five years ago, in Chili, a father was excommunicated for having made his daughters learn the French language: at present, every kind of study is encouraged, all the presses are free; all the states, all the provinces, vie with each other in establishing new seminaries of education. Formerly the culture of the vine and olive tree was prohibited, as well as the production and fabrication of every thing that might be imported from Spain: now every branch of indus-

E

try and commerce is protected; and property increases in value from year to year to an astonishing degree. Formerly, bull fights, with refinements of cruelty, unknown even in Spain, were encouraged by the Germans in all the large towns; and in 1820, Lima then resounded with the wild shouts of joy of men, women, and children, at the sight of the blood; the torments and the agonies of the bulls, the horses and the *Toreadores*, (bull fighters:) now, wherever the patriots have triumphed, they have abolished those brutal spectacles. Formerly, the slavery of the Indians and negroes accustomed man to despise his fellow man, and to abuse the power he had over him: now, all the new republics have enacted laws for the abolition of slavery.

No doubt there remains much yet to be done for those new republics; but all could not be accomplished at once. It would have been absurd and unjust to require of a new government, that it should reach the end almost at the moment of departure. All that can be fairly expected, is, that it should advance and be disposed to continue advancing; it ought not to be blamed for proceeding slowly, if that slowness is commanded by prudence, and if there is danger of establishing nothing by making too rapid innovations.

The new American states find no longer in their government an obstacle to advancement in their noble career, but many still in the people: the ignorance, intolerance and ferocity, with which their ancient masters have impregnated and disgraced their character, cannot be dissipated in a moment. We must expect that the multitude will repel, for some time, many of the benefits with which civilization would bless them; but we must not be discouraged; the tree is planted in a fertile soil, it will blossom and fructify in due time.

By showing how the retrograde system has been, throughout the world, in hostile opposition to virtue, knowledge, and liberty, we do not mean to assert that its supporters intended all the mischief that they have done. Perhaps they were themselves deceived in the same manner that they deceive others, when they affirm that they are not inimical to the improvement of the human race; that they even wish it to be encouraged, but not with too much haste; they will take time to do good, and they would find even eternity too short. They approve of knowledge, provided it be confined to the first class of society, thus depriving even that class of the benefit of emulation, and denying reason to the common people. They profess great zeal for morality; but with such modifications that it may serve the purposes of the rulers, and be binding only on those who are governed.* Perhaps they have deceived their own judgment; but the germs of reason which God has implanted in the minds of men are not always to be thus misdirected. The Supreme Being indicates the road of improvement as the way to happiness; he has given noble faculties to man, and so united them that they must be developed or perish together; he has made man perfectible, that is to say, susceptible of becoming better, but also of becoming worse; and leaving men afterwards to re-act on each other, he has erected a wholesome limit against tyranny, on which humanity rests its hope;

---

* "Speak to the people of their duties, never of their rights," said one of Napoleon's ministers to the editor of a country newspaper. "Since you are writing upon politics," said the same minister on another occasion, "be very careful not to speak of the duties of the government to the people, but insist strongly on the rights of the chief magistrate of the state and his delegates, and on the obedience due from the subject." It was not thus that Sully, Fenelon, Massillon, thought and spoke; those noble models of counsellors, such as kings ought always to have in order to be great and just, and make their people happy. They knew how to make the monarch and his courtiers listen to the firm and severe language of truth. The power that fears knowledge, and will only have servile and obedient machines, wants a *fulcrum* to bear upon, and will succumb in the end.

Note by M. Jullien.

he has ordered, by an infallible decree, that every power which degrades those that are subjected to it, must thereby be weakened and ultimately fall.

J. C. L. DE SISMONDI.